39 ESL Vocabu␣

For Kids (7+)

Jackie Bolen +

Jennifer Booker Smith

Josh Catlett (Editor)

Table of Contents

About the Author: Jackie Bolen

I've been teaching English in South Korea for a decade to every level and type of student and I've taught every age from kindergarten kids to adults. Most of my time has centered around teaching at two universities: five years at a science and engineering school out in the rice paddies of Chungcheongnam-Do, and four years at a major university in Busan where I now teach high level classes for students majoring in English. In my spare time, you can usually find me outside surfing, biking, hiking or on the hunt for the most delicious kimchi I can find.

In case you were wondering what my academic qualifications are, I hold a Master of Arts in Psychology. During my time in Korea I've successfully completed both the Cambridge CELTA and DELTA certification programs. With the combination of almost ten years teaching ESL/EFL learners of all ages and levels, and the more formal teaching qualifications I've obtained, I have a solid foundation on which to offer teaching advice. I truly hope that you find this book useful and would love it if you sent me an email with any questions or feedback that you might have—I'll always take the time to personally respond (wealthyenglishteacher@gmail.com).

More From Jackie Bolen

If you like ESL Warm-Ups for Adults, please leave a review over on Amazon and don't forget to check out my other books at the same time:

The Wealthy English Teacher is a book in which you can learn all about finances for ESL teachers abroad. You can also check out this related website: *Freedom Through Passive Income* (www.freedomthroughpassiveincome.com).

If you're interested in getting the most awesome job in South Korea—which is working at a university—please check out *How to Get a University Job in South Korea.*

If you teach speaking or conversation classes, you'll find two books useful First there is *39 No-Prep/Low-Prep ESL Speaking Activities: For Teenagers and Adults* but there's also the version for children: *39 No-Prep/Low-Prep ESL Speaking Activities: For Kids (7+).*

Jackie Bolen Around the Internet

ESL Speaking (www.eslspeaking.org)

Jackie Bolen (www.jackiebolen.com)

Twitter: @bolen_jackie

About the Author: Jennifer Booker Smith

I have a Master of Education in TESOL and have spent fifteen years teaching students of all ages in Korea, from two-year-old preschoolers barely out of diapers to businessmen and even a semester as a teacher trainer at an education university. However, my greatest love is the middle primary grades—I left a fairly cushy teacher trainer position to return to the elementary classroom. In that age group, I've taught all ability levels from false beginner to near-native returnees.

During my time in the classroom, I've created countless board and card games and other resources. In this book, you'll find some of the vocabulary activities that I have used successfully (I've tried plenty which weren't successful!) in a variety of settings; these are the ones I've used again and again because they get students talking and they actually work.

When I'm not teaching, like Jackie, you can often find me hiking. I've taken up running recently and will soon be running my third half marathon. Teaching takes up a lot more "free" time than non-teachers will ever realize, so it's important to recharge the batteries and being outside is my favorite way to do just that.

You can get in touch with me by emailing jenniferteacher@gmail.com. I'd love to hear from you and help you with your classes in any way that I can, particularly if you have a difficult children's class and would like some advice about that. I'll do my best to assist you.

About the Editor: Josh Catlett

After graduating with a bachelor's degree in English, I worked in a few different fields that included everything from technical writing at a national media company to human resources at a small startup company focused on green energy. At a certain point, though, I realized I'd entered a vicious cycle of living to work and working to live.

I quit my job, moved to Miami for a few months to earn my CELTA and then moved to South Korea to begin teaching English. I now focus on the things that make me happy: teaching, discussing literature and movies, reading about new technologies, writing/editing, playing board games with friends and traveling.

I'm always on the lookout for new writing or editing assignments, so if you'd like to work together on something you can drop me a line at joshua.catlett@gmail.com. I look forward to hearing from you!

Games and Activities for All Levels

Basketball Vocabulary Challenge

Skills: Listening/Speaking

Time: 10-15 minutes

Age: 7+

Materials: Empty trash can, "balls"

This is a fun game that children love! You can play with the entire class if you have fewer than eight students or in teams if you have more, but you need a big space to play it such as a large classroom with few desks, gymnasium or outside. Place the empty trash can in the middle of the open space. Arrange the students around the room as far from the basket as possible (touching the wall, behind the chalk line, etc.) and give each student a ball. They can be real balls, but I find that a piece of scrunched up scrap paper works best. Then, place a line of flashcards in front of each person leading toward the basket. Five per player works well.

Going in order one student at a time, the students have two choices: aim for the basket or say the vocabulary word on the flashcard immediately in front of them and move up closer to the basket. If they aim for the basket but miss, they are out of the game and must go sit down. If they say the word correctly, they move up closer and wait until the next round when they have the same decision. If they say the wrong word, they are also out of the game. Continue in a circle until all the players are out of the game, either because they missed a shot, got a shot in the basket or said a vocabulary word incorrectly. You can give a point or small prize to the first player to get a shot in the basket.

An optional variation is to give different points for various shots as you would in a regular basketball game. For example, from flashcards #5/4 = 3 points. Flashcards #3/2 = 2 points. Flashcard #1 = 1 point.

Procedure:

1. Place an empty trash cash in the center of a large playing area.

2. Arrange five flashcards per student leading from the perimeter to the basket.

3. Line students up at the perimeter behind a row of flashcards. Each student has to be holding a ball of some kind.

4. Students take turns in order and have two choices. The first choice is to shoot their ball at the basket. If they miss, they are out of the game. If they make the basket, they get a point. The other choice is to say the word on the flashcard closest to them and if correct, they move up to that location and waits until their next turn. If incorrect, they are out of the game.

5. The winner is the first student(s) to score a basket. Or, if you're giving different points for the various shots, you can play 3-5 rounds and add up the scores from each round.

Boggle

Skills: Writing

Time: 10 minutes

Age: 8+

Materials: "Boggle" grid on PowerPoint, whiteboard/paper

You've probably played the word game Boggle before: you shake up the letters and then you have a certain amount of time to make some words with connecting letters. You can play it with your students, but you don't need the actual Boggle game. Simply make up a grid on the whiteboard, PowerPoint or on a piece of paper. I make a 6x6 grid and put some obvious words in like the names of colors or animals, or the vocabulary that we've recently been studying. Then, students divide into pairs and have to make as many words as possible that are 4+ letters. You can give a bonus for longer words if you like. At the end, students count up how many points they have. You can double check for any errors and then award a small prize to the winning team.

Procedure:

1. Prepare a "Boggle" grid.

2. Divide students into pairs and try to make as many words as possible with 4+ letters. Students cannot use the same letter in a single square twice within a single word.

3. Students add up points. The teacher checks the answers of the top two or three teams.

o	r	p	t	s	a
e	a	i	e	t	f
b	k	n	e	r	i
a	d	r	g	o	r
c	o	t	l	s	e
k	f	h	m	a	n

Some possible words from this board:

green, pink, rake, back, fire, fires, fast, road, rose

Concentratlon

Skills: Reading

Time: 10-15 minutes

Age: 7+

Materials: Concentration cards

This is a memory game designed to help students remember vocabulary words and definitions. Make up sets of cards with words on half the cards and the matching definition on the other half. A total of 16 cards (8 sets of words and definitions) works well. Make enough cards so that there is one set for each group of four students.

Students mix up the cards and put them face down on the desk in an organized fashion. The students play rocks-scissors-paper. The first student chooses two cards and places them face up on the desk so that everyone is able to see them. If they make a set, the student keeps the cards (they're removed from the game), gets one point and is able to choose again. If they don't make a set, the student places them face-down in the **same spot** (it's a memory game!) and the game continues with the next student.

Procedure:

1. Make concentration card sets of words and definitions (16 cards per set, one set per four students).

2. Have students mix the cards and place them face down on the desk in an organized manner.

3. The first student chooses two cards and places them face up on the desk. If they make a set, the student keeps the cards and gets one point. If they don't make a set, the student places them face down in the same spot and the game continues with the next student who reveals two more cards.

4. The winner is the student with the most points.

Correction Relay

Skill: Reading/Writing

Time: 10+ minutes

Age: 9+

Materials: Worksheet

This is an activity that uses speed and competition to make something old (error correction) new again. Students of all levels should be quite familiar with finding and correcting errors in sentences. By adding a relay aspect, it will (hopefully) make an important but sometimes tedious skill new and more interesting.

To prepare the activity, create a worksheet with 10-15 errors. You can focus your errors on one aspect of vocabulary, such as synonyms and antonyms, or more simply, misuse vocabulary words in sentences. For lower level students, limit the errors to one per sentence. Higher levels can handle multiple errors in one sentence, and you can increase the challenge by having one vocabulary error per sentence and one or more other errors, such as grammar or punctuation mistakes.

The activity itself is straightforward. Students will work in teams of 4-5 to correct the worksheet as quickly as possible. Each student makes one correction and passes the worksheet to the next person who makes the next correction. They continue to pass the worksheet around until it is complete. You can make it easier by allowing students to choose any remaining sentence to correct, or you can require them to work from top to bottom.

Teaching Tips:

To prevent one student from carrying the rest of the team, do not allow other team members to correct another correction. That is, a sentence cannot be corrected by a second student once someone has corrected it. This also prevents more assertive (but not necessarily more able) students from incorrectly correcting others' work.

Also, to keep things moving along you may want to have a time limit for each turn before students must pass the worksheet along.

Procedure:

1. In advance, prepare a worksheet with 10-15 sentences containing vocabulary errors.
2. Divide students into groups of 4-5. If possible, group the desks to facilitate easy passing of the worksheets.
3. Have students take turns making one correction and passing the worksheet to the next student to make one correction. They continue passing and correcting until the worksheet is complete.
4. When all teams are finished, go over the errors as a class. The team with the most correct sentences wins.

Disappearing Words

Skills: Reading

Time: 10 minutes

Age: 7+

Materials: Whiteboard

This vocabulary game is an easy way to force students to keep a set of new vocabulary words in their heads or to review past words. Write down 10-15 words on the whiteboard and give students 1-2 minutes to study them. Then, if you have a big class, ask everyone to close their eyes as you choose one or two words to erase. Students open their eyes and have to tell you what is missing and where it was. If you have a small class, you can choose individual students to close their eyes and then tell you the missing word(s) after you've erased them. You can either write those words in their spots again or add new words to the mix and continue the game.

Procedure:

1. Write down 10-15 vocabulary words on the whiteboard.

2. Have student(s) close their eyes as you erase 1-2 words.

3. Students open their eyes and tell you which words are missing and where they were.

4. You can write those same words back in or add new words to the mix in those same spots and continue the game.

Flyswatter

Skills: Listening/Reading

Time: 5-10 minutes

Age: 7+

Materials: Whiteboard, 2 flyswatters

This is a game that can really energize your class at the end of a long day or semester. It makes an excellent way to review any new vocabulary that you've taught or as a warm-up at the beginning of the next class. Write the target words on the board in a random fashion. You can use 10-20 depending on the age and level of students. Divide the students into two teams. One person from each team comes up to the whiteboard and each person is given a flyswatter. Give hints to describe one of the words and the first student to hit the word with the flyswatter gets a point for his/her team. If two students go for a word at the same time, the one on the bottom of the flyswatter stack gets the point. If a student makes an incorrect choice, he/she is out (no second chances). I usually start with a very general hint and progress to more specific ones where the answer is quite obvious. It's up to the student whether or not he/she wants to risk it and guess before the answer is apparent to everyone.

Procedure:

1. Divide students into two teams.

2. Write 10-20 vocabulary words on the whiteboard in random fashion.

3. The first two students come to the board and are each given a flyswatter.

4. The teacher gives hints for one of the words, starting with general ones and getting more specific.

5. The student hits the word with his/her flyswatter when he/she knows the answer.

6. If correct, his/her team gets a point and the next two students come to the board. If

incorrect, the other student is given a chance to guess the word and the teacher can give more hints if necessary. If both students are incorrect, both will sit down and neither team gets a point.

Human Logic Puzzle

Skills: Listening/Speaking/Writing

Time: 5-10 minutes

Age: 7-11

Materials: Flashcards, answer grids

You probably remember logic puzzles from when you were a kid. It begins with a short story followed by clues and a grid for keeping track of the information. In this activity, there are clues but no short story.

In advance, prepare a grid with the terms you want to review. The terms should be listed across the top while blanks for student names should be along the side. With lower-level students, you may want to use this for jobs, animals, actions or other terms the students will be able to provide clues for fairly easily. With higher-level students, you can use a broader variety of vocabulary and they can give synonyms, antonyms and/or definitions.

Before you begin, you need to select student helpers/clue providers to go to the front of the class. Give each two flashcards, and tell them not to show anyone. Give the rest of the students the answer grid and tell them to write the student helpers' names.

In turn, student helpers/clue providers should give one clue about one of their flashcards. For something like jobs, they can describe where the person works, what they do, etc. For animals or actions, they can act it out and/or make noises. Let the students give the first round of clues themselves while subsequent rounds will include audience participation. That is, the "audience" asks questions. Continue until one student has correctly completed his/her grid.

Variations:

To make it more challenging:

1. Limit students to two turns, i.e. one turn per flash card. If no one has correctly completed his/her grid, students could then work in pairs or small groups.

2. Have two columns on the answer sheet, rather than a grid, so students will write the names of the students and the vocabulary they are describing.

To make it less challenging:

1. Have students continue giving more clues until everyone has completed their grid.

2. Have students work in small groups or pairs. Give them 15-20 seconds between clues to discuss.

Procedure:

1. In advance, prepare a grid with the terms you want to review.

2. Select student helpers/clue providers to go to the front of the class and give each of them two flashcards.

3. Give the rest of the class the answer grid and tell them to write the student helpers' names.

4. Have student helpers/clue providers give one clue about one of their flashcards in turn. After they have given one clue about each flashcard, the clues should be responses to student questions. (You may want to make rules about the questions they can ask.)

5. Give the class time to think and write between each clue.

6. Students continue giving clues until one student has correctly filled out their grid.

Musical Flashcards

Skills: Speaking

Time: 5 minutes

Age: 6-11

Materials: Flashcards (large enough for the entire class to see), music.

Optional Materials: Timer, second set of flashcards, monitor/overhead projector

Some days, kids are just too antsy to focus especially when the weather is bad and they haven't been able to play at recess. This is good for getting the kids moving around the classroom while still focusing on English.

To set up, have students stand behind their seats with the chair pushed in. Explain to them that as the music plays, they should move in a circle around the class. When the music stops, they stop. You will show them a card. The students must say what it is. If they cannot say it, then they are out and must sit down.

Start the music. Let it play from 5-15 seconds (switch it up each time). Stop the music and quickly show a flashcard. You can go through your deck one at a time and create a discard pile, or you can randomly choose and have some repeats. To make it harder, literally flash the card: show it to the entire class, but for only a few seconds.

Have the students name the flashcard together. If a student doesn't know the word or is too slow to see the flashcard you've shown, then they are out and must sit down.

Variations:

No one gets out, but you need a second set of flashcards. Lay one flashcard on each student desk. Discard any from your deck that are not used. Whoever is in front of that card when you flash it must hold it up and say it. For example, if you hold up a flashcard of an apple, the student standing in front of the desk with the apple flashcard must hold it up and say, "Apple."

For higher-level students, you can have them make a sentence or give the definition, rather than simply say the word.

Teaching Tips:

Unless your class is very small, your students will probably not have a neat circle to move around. So, before you begin, take them on a practice lap or two with you leading the way. To do this, pick a starting point (desk) and have everyone follow you as you move from desk to desk around the entire class. What is important is that they see which direction to move in and where to go when leaving one group of desks or row and joining another.

If you have a large classroom, your set of flashcards should be large enough for the entire class to see. I use A4 flashcards. Another option is to have PowerPoint slides of each card or an overhead projector. If you make your own flashcards, you are probably making them in PPT anyway. If you've made them in portrait, convert them to landscape. There will be a wide border on the left and right, but the image will still be large enough to see.

To keep things moving, I give a 3-finger countdown and have everyone answer together. This game isn't fun indefinitely, so you want to try to cut several students each round.

Procedure:

1. In advance, prepare a set of flashcards and music.

2. To set up, have students stand behind their seat with their chair pushed in.

3. Explain to them that as they music plays, they should move in a circle around the class. When the music stops, they stop. You will show them a card. The students must say what it is. If they cannot say it, they are out and must sit down.

4. Start the music. Let it play from 5-15 seconds (switch it up each time).

5. Stop the music and quickly hold up a flashcard.

6. If a student can't name the flashcard you've shown, they are out and must sit down.

7. Repeat until there is only one student remaining.

Name 5 Things

Skills: Listening/Writing

Time: 5 minutes

Age: 8+

Materials: Paper, pencil

This is an excellent warm-up activity at the beginning of class to review vocabulary words from the previous class. Put students into pairs. They'll need one piece of paper and one pen. Tell them to name five _____. The category will depend on the level and age of students. For beginners, you could do easy things like animals, colors, fruits, etc. For higher-level students, you could use things that move, animals with four legs, things that can fly, breakfast foods, etc. The first team to write down their five things raises their hands and you can check to make sure all the answers are appropriate.

Procedure:

1. Put students into pairs with one piece of paper and one pencil.

2. Tell the class to, "Name five _____." Each team has to write down five words on their paper.

3. Once a team is finished, they raise their hands.

4. Check to make sure all the team's answers are appropriate.

Odd One Out

Skills: Reading/Speaking or Writing

Time: 5 minutes

Age: 8+

Materials: Groups of words

You can use Odd One Out to review vocabulary from previous classes. Write a few sets of vocabulary words on the whiteboard. I use four in one group, with one of them being the "odd one out" (meaning it's not like the others). For example: orange, cucumber, apple, banana. Cucumber is the odd one out because it's not a fruit.

Procedure:

1. Make 4-6 groups of four words with one word in each group being unlike the others.

2. Put students in pairs and have them choose the odd word from each group and also write (or say) why they chose it. For example: Cucumber-not a fruit.

Puzzles

Skills: Reading/Writing

Time: 10-30 minutes

Age: 7+

Materials: A word puzzle

Puzzles are an excellent way to review vocabulary and I find that most students enjoy doing them, particularly teenagers. They can also work very well for "quiet" classes that don't have a lot of outgoing students in them where it's hard to do some of the more active games like charades. It's really easy to make puzzles yourself using something like Discovery.com's Puzzle maker (www.discoveryeducation.com/free-puzzlemaker), and it's actually the preferable option since you can include all the specific vocabulary that you'd like. I prefer to use the criss-cross option. It has the most educational benefit since it deals with meanings as well as vocabulary words.

Procedure:

1. Go to Discovery.com and find the puzzle maker.

2. Design your puzzle (criss-cross is best!), using words and definitions. Alternatively, you can give hints about the word related to the context you'd use it in instead of the actual definition. Here are two examples:

This animal has black and white stripes (skunk).

If a _____ sprays you, you'll smell really bad (skunk).

3. Have students complete the puzzle. I usually make it a bit competitive by putting them in pairs and awarding the first couple of teams a prize of some sort.

4. It's up to you whether or not to allow dictionaries or textbooks. In my experience, dictionaries don't really help that much whereas the course book where the words came from really does. You could also say that for the first five minutes, they must only use their brains, but they can use anything they want after that. If there is a particularly hard one that no student is able to get, I'll give the entire class a hint.

Q&A

Skill: Speaking/Writing
Time: 10 minutes
Age: 9+
Materials: Nothing

This is a simple variation on having students make example sentences using their vocabulary list. Students work in pairs of teams creating a list of WH questions (to avoid yes/no answers) using their vocabulary words. When they have five questions, teams should alternate asking a question to another team and answering the other team's questions.

You can extend the activity with some reported speech practice, which will give teams an incentive to listen to the responses to their questions.

Procedure:

1. Divide students into an even number of teams of 2-4. Then pair two teams together.

2. Give students a few minutes to create five WH questions using their vocabulary words.

3. Have the paired teams alternate asking and answering each other's questions.

4. Optionally, extend the activity by having teams briefly report the other team's answers.

QR Code Hunt

Skills: Speaking/Listening

Time: 15-30 minutes

Age: 10+

Materials: Internet access, printer, tape/Blu-tack, student phones with QR code reader apps installed, list of vocabulary words

This activity requires a bit more prep than others, but (as of writing) the novelty factor is high enough to draw some students In who might otherwise be too cool for school. Classtools.net makes it easy to put together a QR code hunt, so don't worry if you haven't used QR codes before—if you can type, you can do this activity.

Teaching Tips:

You can go in a few different directions with this activity, and a pub quiz is a light-hearted way to get students talking. Just make sure the questions aren't so obscure that your students spend the class googling the answers! The younger the students, the narrower the scope of your trivia questions has to be. Recent blockbuster movies, popular games, current pop stars, big sporting events, etc. are all things that work well, but they will have to be updated every semester.

Procedure:

1. In advance, write a list of questions using the vocabulary list in a Word document. These can be discussion questions, trivia questions (pub quiz), or they can pre-test student levels, particularly if you are teaching a subject class.

2. Go to www.classtools.net/QR and copy and paste.

3. Create the QR codes and print.

4. Post the printouts in various places around the class, or better yet, a larger area.

5. Before dividing students into groups, make sure at least one member of each group has a QR reader on his/her phone. If not, give them a minute to download an app—there are plenty and many students will already have one.

6. Divide students into groups of 3-4 and give them a time limit to find and answer all of the questions.

7. Optionally, particularly if you plan to assess student levels, you can have students write the questions they find, along with their answers.

8. Wrap up with a discussion of the answers.

Review Race

Skill: Writing

Time: 5 minutes

Age: 9+

Materials: Large paper (one piece per group)/whiteboard and markers (at least one per group)

Some students tend to look at each lesson as a discrete unit and forget that they are parts of a whole. This activity gets them using what they have learned. It's a great warm-up activity. I've also used it before a test, both to boost their confidence and to give them one last bit of review time.

Divide students into groups of 4-5 and give each group at least one marker. If you are not using a whiteboard, give each group one piece of A3 or butcher paper. Give students a time limit of 2-3 minutes to list all of the vocabulary words they can remember from the previous lesson. With higher-level classes, have students add a synonym, antonym or brief definition. The group with the most correct words wins.

Procedure:

1. In advance, prepare markers and optionally a piece of A3 or butcher paper for each group.

2. Divide students into groups of 4-5.

3. Have students work together to list all of the vocabulary words they can remember from the previous lesson within the time limit of 2-3 minutes.

4. For higher-level classes, have students add a synonym, antonym or brief definition of each word.

5. The group with the most correct words wins.

Rock, Scissors, Paper: Tell it Walking

Skills: Reading/Speaking

Time: 5 minutes

Age: 7-11

Materials: Flashcards

This is a good, short review to do at the beginning of class. Not every student will get to participate, so you may want to keep track of who has had a chance to play if you intend to play regularly.

To set up the activity, place the flashcards along the whiteboard eraser ledge or on the whiteboard. Choose two students to "duel." They will each start at opposite ends of the whiteboard. To play, they will take one step and say the flashcard, then take another step and repeat. When the two students meet, they will play RSP for the right to name that flashcard. The loser goes back to the beginning and the winner continues. When one student makes it to the other's starting point, they win.

Variation:

If you have the floor space, have all students work in pairs. Give each pair a set of flashcards (they do not need to be the same set), and tell them to lay them on the floor in a line that they walk beside. The rest is played the same. If each group has a different set of flashcards, have students exchange cards to play more rounds.

Teaching Tips:

Students must take a step that matches the spacing of the cards in order to read each card.

Students do not work at a synchronized pace—the faster reader/speaker will get farther than the slower reader/speaker.

Procedure:

1. In advance, prepare a set of flashcards. Display them on the whiteboard or along the eraser ledge.

2. Choose two students to duel and have each stand at opposite ends of the flashcards.

3. To play, they will take one step and say the flashcard, then take another step and repeat. The length of their steps should be the distance between flashcards.

4. When the two students meet, they will play RSP for the right to name that flashcard.

5. The loser goes back to the beginning and the winner continues.

6. When one student makes it to the other's starting point, that student is the winner.

Scoot

Skills: Reading/Writing

Time: 20+ minutes

Age: 7-11

Materials: Flashcards (you will need to number them) or task cards, timer, answer sheets

If you haven't played Scoot before, it's a fun way to get kids moving. Because there is a time limit and they are moving, they don't feel like the exercises are such a chore. If you haven't used task cards before, they are flashcard-sized cards with one "task" on each one. The task can be whatever you want them to practice, everything from unscrambling vocabulary words to alphabetizing to sentence correction and so on.

To play, lay one card face down on each desk. Give students an answer sheet or have them use their notebooks. When you start the timer, they turn over the cards and record their answers. When timer rings, they turn the card back over and move to the next seat. Repeat until they have gone around the room and are back in their own seats.

The age and the level of the students will affect what type of tasks you can use for Scoot. For lower-level students, use multiple choice activities, such as choosing the correct spelling of a vocabulary word (with or without a picture), alphabetical order of three words or syllable division. For advanced students, the task may be to write the definition of a given word or an original sentence. Whatever you are teaching, you can create task cards to complement the lesson.

Teaching Tips:

If students are using their notebooks, have them write the numbers before you begin. Otherwise, some of them will just write answers from top to bottom and end up with an answer sheet that looks like this: 8, 3, 12, 25, 1. . .

Unless your class is very small, your students will probably not have a neat circle to move around. So, before you begin, take them on a practice lap or two, with you leading the way. To do this, pick a starting point (desk) and have everyone follow you as you move from desk to desk around the entire class. What is important is that they see which direction to move in and where to go when leaving one group of desks or row and joining another.

The time you give for each round is up to you. It should be long enough to read and answer, but short enough that students feel a bit like they are racing the clock.

Procedure:

1. In advance, prepare a set of flashcards or task cards and a timer. You may also want to prepare answer sheets, or you can have students use their notebooks.

2. To begin, lay one card face down on each desk.

3. Give students an answer sheet or have them use their notebooks.

4. When you start the timer, they turn over the card and record their answer.

5. When timer rings, they turn the card back over and move to the next seat.

6. Repeat until they have gone around the room and are back in their own seats.

7. You can check answers together if there is only one correct answer possible, or you can collect them.

Scrabble

Skill: Writing

Time: 20+ minutes

Age: 9+

Materials: Oversized wall-mounted board/one board per table, letter set

Your students will likely be familiar with Scrabble, either the board game or similar apps. It's a great way to get students to recall vocabulary and use correct spelling. It's a bit labor intensive to create the board(s), but I get several years of use out of a wall-mounted board.

To make a wall-mounted board, I use a large (big enough for letters to be seen across the classroom) piece of felt. Thin quilt batting is not as durable but may be easier to come by. The Velcro on the back of the letters will pull bits of it off, but I still can get enough use out of a board to make it a viable option. I use an actual board as a guide for number of squares and arrangement of "special" squares, but I add in a few more than in the standard game. Wikipedia has the official list of number of letters and point values, which I use as well. I make the letter cards about the size of my hand so that the words can be read across the classroom. I laminate them (of course!) and stick a square of "pointy" Velcro on the back. Since the board is felt or batting, the Velcro sticks right on.

If the class is lower-level, I have the students work in pairs or threes. If the class is quite large, I use table-top game boards. You can splurge and pay for real boards, but I just use A3 paper. I make a top board and bottom board, print them, cut off the border at the join, laminate them, and tape them together. You will need a set of letters of the appropriate size, but you don't need Velcro.

Teaching Tips:

To increase the challenge, you can limit them to words they have studied, for example, as a semester review. However, the game itself is likely to be challenging enough. In fact, I usually give a bonus of one point per letter, and sometimes a further bonus for 6+ letter words, to encourage longer words.

Procedure:

1. In advance, prepare one wall-mounted board with letter cards with Velcro on the back, or enough game boards and letter sets for each table to have one. (I use Wikipedia for the game board layout and letter point values and numbers.)

2. Depending on class size and level, have students work as individuals, pairs, or threes. (A large class playing as individuals on a wall-mounted board will create a lot of downtime.)

3. You may want to give bonuses for longer words. If necessary, start a new word in a corner of the board or add a long word of your own if there is a large number of 3-4 letter words.

Stack Attack

Skills: Reading/Speaking

Time: 5+ minutes

Age: 6-11

Materials: Flashcards (one set per pair), small cups (same number as flash cards, plus three or four for a tower base), timer

This is a speed activity. Each round is 30-60 seconds (have longer rounds for more words, or shorter for fewer). In this activity, students work in pairs: one student shows the second student a flashcard and the second student names it. With each word, they should add one cup to their tower. If either of the following happens, the student must start over (both the tower and the stack of flash cards):

1. Students do not say the word correctly or do not know the word (his/her partner should give them the correct answer, so that they can do it the next time.)

2. Their tower falls over.

When the timer goes off, the two students switch roles. The student in each pair whose tower was the tallest wins. You can extend the game with knockout rounds until there is one winner for the class, or you can have students play again with the same partner or a new one.

Variation:

Higher level students can make a sentence or give the definition, rather than (or in addition to) saying the word. Give them enough flashcards for a 90-120 second round.

Teaching Tips:

This one is good for younger kids, but your 9-11 year olds may like it as well. I use the little cups used for dispensing medicine. Sleeves of disposable coffee cups from the school office can work well too. The younger the students, the larger the cup you may want to use. I've also used empty toilet rolls for this, which adds a bit of challenge because they are harder to balance.

Procedure:

1. In advance, prepare one set of flashcards per pair of students, plus a stack of small cups of 3-4 more than the number of flashcards.

2. Have students create a tower base with the extra 3-4 cups by setting them upside down side by side.

3. Set the timer for 30-60 seconds.

4. Have the students work in pairs, with one showing the flashcards one at a time and the other reading it and then stacking one cup on their tower.

5. Students must start over if they do not know the word or if their tower falls.

6. If a student doesn't know a word, their partner should tell them before they start over.

7. When the timer goes off, the pair switches roles.

Synonym/Antonym Brainstorm Race

Skill: Writing

Time: 5 minutes

Age: 8+

Materials: Large paper (one piece per group)/whiteboard and markers (at least one per group)

This is similar to the Review Race game, but is used with new vocabulary after introducing the terms and definitions. To play, divide students into groups of 4-5 and give each group at least one marker. If you are not using the whiteboard, also give each group one piece of A3 or butcher paper. Give students a time limit of 2-3 minutes to list all of the vocabulary words they can remember from the previous lesson. With higher-level classes, have students add a synonym, antonym or brief definition. The group with the most correct words wins.

Procedure:

1. In advance, prepare markers and optionally, a piece of A3 or butcher paper for each group.

2. Divide students into groups of 4-5.

3. Have students work together to list all of the vocabulary and add at least one synonym and antonym of each word.

4. The group with the most correct words wins.

Vocabulary Square

Skill: Writing

Time: 20+ minutes

Age: 9+

Materials: Index cards (students should be told in advance to bring one card per vocabulary word); dictionary/textbook with glossary

This is a class activity to facilitate self study as well as dictionary skills. Many students these days rely on their electronic dictionaries for translations and don't develop their English-English dictionary skills. They may also not realize the benefits of flashcards for vocabulary self study. Regular repetition of exposure to new words is necessary to commit them to working memory.

It is an easy activity to set up. Have students divide their index cards into four corners:

1. Write the meaning in the students' own words.

2. Write at least one synonym and one antonym.

3. Write an example sentence.

4. Draw an image representing the term.

Remind students to review the flashcards at least once a day.

Teaching Tips:

You may want to complete a few examples together to remind students to restate the definitions rather than copying them. A PowerPoint of a completed index card will help students more easily understand the task. You could also draw an example on the whiteboard.

Procedure:

1. At least one class in advance, tell students to bring index cards. Alternatively, you can cut copy paper into 8 pieces (but copy paper is not as durable).

2. Explain to students that flashcards are a great way to learn new vocabulary if they review the cards often.

3. Have students divide their index cards into four corners and fill as follows:

1. Write the meaning in the students' own words.

2. Write at least one synonym and one antonym.

3. Write an example sentence.

4. Draw an image representing the term.

Vocabulary Pictionary

Skills: Speaking/Listening

Time: 10-15 minutes

Age: 8+

Materials: Whiteboard, marker, eraser

Optional Materials: Flash-cards

This is a great review game with no preparation required. Divide students into teams and choose which team will go first. That team will choose a representative to go to the whiteboard and he/she will have to draw pictures (I use a pile of flashcards) that his/her team guesses. The goal is to get as many points as possible in a specified amount of time (two minutes). Then, the next team does the same thing. You can play as many rounds as you want.

I use this with classes of up to 40 students, and it works well as long as no one gets too rowdy. In those large classes, have students sit at tables, rather than individual desks, so that they can work together easily. If you have a large class seated at desks, you should arrange them into groups of 4-8 desks depending on class size. If you have a class of ten or fewer, just divide them into two teams.

Procedure:

1. Divide students into equal teams of 4-8. Have each team choose a representative to draw.

2. Demonstrate by drawing a picture representing a familiar term on the whiteboard and elicit guesses from the students.

3. The team that correctly guesses the word will go first. The other team representatives will play rock-scissors-paper to determine their order.

4. Have the drawer from the first team go to the whiteboard and show him/her a flashcard.

He/she has to draw it.

5. As he/she draws, his/her team guesses the correct word. The drawer takes another card and the team continues to guess. Continue until the specified time is up.

6. Continue until each team has had at least one chance to play.

Word Association

Skills: Reading/Writing/Speaking

Time: 5 minutes

Age: 8+

Materials: Whiteboard, markers/butcher (or A3) paper, pens

To introduce a new vocabulary word, write it in the middle of the board or paper and have students take turns adding as many words or images related to that word as possible. For large classes, have students work in groups with separate pieces of paper taped to the wall or the top of the table/grouped desks. After a given amount of time (2 3 minutes, or when you see no one is adding anything new), discuss their answers.

Teaching Tips:

For large classes, butcher paper works best because more students can write at one time. If that isn't possible, have 5-6 board markers available.

If you're using butcher paper, prepare in advance by taping it to the wall unless students will be working at their desks. If students will be working at their desks, write the word on each table's page in advance, but don't hand them out until you have given your instructions.

Procedure:

1. Write a single new vocabulary word on the whiteboard or butcher paper.

2. Have students take turns adding as many words or images related to that word as possible.

3. After 2-3 minutes (or less, if no one is adding anything new), discuss their answers.

Word of the Day

Skills: Writing

Time: 5 minutes

Age: 7+

Materials: Whiteboard/PowerPoint

I have frequently been required to give my students a word, quote, or idiom of the day, outside of our usual text but generally related to the text or a monthly theme. You can easily start a Word of the Day activity for your students by giving them a single word each day from their text (but not a vocabulary word), current events or by having a theme for each month.

Write the word on the whiteboard or PowerPoint along with the definition, part of speech, and several example sentences. Have students copy all of this in their notebooks in a section for their Words of the Day. You can use the word as an exit ticket, have a weekly quiz, or add one or two words to each regular vocabulary quiz.

Variation (more advanced):

Idiom of the Day is where you give students an idiom with a definition and a picture (if possible). Have them make 1-3 sentences using it correctly.

Procedure:

1. In advance, prepare a collection of words from your students' textbook but not part of the vocabulary list.

2. Begin each day (or one day per week) with one new word. Introduce the word just as you would their regular vocabulary: present the word, the definition, part of speech and several example sentences.

3. Have students copy the sentences in the notebooks and add their own sentence.

4. Add all or some Words of the Day to your regular vocabulary quizzes.

Words in Words

Skills: Writing

Time: 5-10 minutes

Age: 7+

Materials: Worksheet/Whiteboard/PowerPoint

You probably did this when you were in school. Give students a word and have them make as many words as possible using the letters in that word. For example: "vacation" = a, on, no, act, action, taco, ant, van. You can give a point for each word so that the student with the most words wins, or you can give more points for longer words. When time is up (about five minutes), show students the possible answers.

Wordles.com has a tool that allows you to type in a word and get the possible words. For vacation, they listed 45 words, some of which I should have thought of myself and some of which are "Scrabble words." Since your students will not possibly know all of these words, it is up to you whether you show all the answers or an abridged list.

For an example of what this activity looks like, go to: www.teacherspayteachers.com/Product/Freebie-Halloween-Words-in-Words-Activity-Color-Version-2164062.

Procedure:

1. In advance, prepare a long word and write it on the whiteboard or a PowerPoint or give students individual worksheets.

2. Give students a time limit of about five minutes to make words from the letters in the word.

3. To make it a competition, when time is up you can give students points for each word.

4. When the activity is finished, show students all of the possible words they could have made. You can get these from www.wordles.com.

You're an Artist!

Skills: Listening

Time: 5-10 minutes

Age: 7-11

Materials: Whiteboard, markers

This is a fun way for children to show off their artistic skills while reviewing some vocabulary at the same time. Kids (and adults) love writing on the whiteboard so students seem to really enjoy this activity. It's best played with small classes of fewer than eight students so that everyone can draw at the same time, but if you have a large class you can make it into a team competition. Have the students arrange themselves behind the student at the board in lines and play enough rounds so that everyone is able to draw at least once.

The way it works is that each student has a box on the whiteboard with his/her name above it (or team name). You call out a word, either simple nouns like "banana" or "dog," or phrases like, "A man is running" or "The student is studying." Give the students a set amount of time (1-2 minutes) to draw their picture and then you can judge their artwork and declare the winner of that round.

Procedure:

1.Have students line up at the board. Each student has a square to draw in with his/her name at the top and a marker.

2.Call out a word or phrase and the students have to draw it in a certain amount of time (1-2 minutes).

3. Judge who has the best picture at the end of the round.

Games and Activities for Lower-Level Students

Disappearing Text

Skills: Reading/Speaking

Time: 5-10 minutes

Age: 7+

Materials: Whiteboard, marker, eraser

This is a good filler activity to practice vocabulary and grammar. Write one (or more) sentences on the board reviewing new material from that class, or from the previous class if you're using this as a warm-up activity.

This can be done as last man standing or last group/table standing. Begin with all students standing. Have them read aloud what is written on the board. Remove one word (or phrase) at a time, and have them repeat the entire passage as it was originally written. As students make mistakes, they must sit down and are out of the game. The winner is the student or table that remains standing the longest. If you are using this as a filler activity, you can stretch the game by playing more than one round.

Teaching Tips:

Before you begin, let students know the order of play (table 1, table 2, from left to right, front to back, etc.) to keep things moving along in an orderly fashion. If the game seems too easy, remove more elements at one time (for example, two words instead of one), or in random order. On the other hand, if it seems more difficult than you expected, remove items in order (from beginning to end or end to beginning.)

If you have more than about 15 students, you should have them play in teams according to the seating arrangement (pairs/groups/tables). When one person on the team makes a mistake, then the entire group is out. This will shorten each round considerably. Since students are less likely to be engaged once they are out, you will want to keep things moving.

Procedure:

1. Write a sentence on the whiteboard. Optionally, have a PowerPoint prepared.

2. Have the entire class stand and read aloud what is on the board.

3. Erase one word or phrase at a time and have the class repeat the sentence in its entirety.

4. Anyone who makes an error must sit down, until there is one student, group or table left standing.

Hidden Object Pictures

Skill: Speaking

Time: 10+ minutes

Age: 7+

Materials: Worksheet, crayons/markers

You may remember hidden object pictures from your childhood. If you haven't done this before, it is a drawing with a number of objects "hidden" in the picture. Obviously, it is best suited to teaching nouns. Students should work in pairs or small groups, discussing the picture as they look for the list of objects. In any case, you don't want your students to sit silently for an entire class period coloring.

Teaching Tips:

If you want to make sure each person has a fairly equal amount of speaking practice, give each member of the group a part of the list. This will force students to ask each other what objects are on the other lists.

If you decide to have students color, then you don't need a full set of crayons or markers for each student. Put two complete sets in baskets or cups for each table to share.

Procedure:

1. In advance, prepare a hidden object picture worksheet (there are many available for free online) and, optionally, bring sufficient crayons or markers for the class.

2. Begin with a brief review of the vocabulary related to the hidden items.

3. Divide students into groups of 2-4 and have them work together to find the hidden images.

4. Finish by having students show their pictures and naming the images they have found. You can extend the task by having students describe the main image as well.

Last Person Standing

Skills: Speaking/Listening

Time: 5-10 minutes

Age: 6+

Materials: Nothing

Choose a topic based on whatever you're teaching. Some examples are jobs, food, animals, things in the kitchen or classroom, etc. Have all the students stand up in a circle. Clap your hands in a beat 1-2-3 and say a word related to that topic. Continue the 1-2-3 rhythm and have the next person in the circle say a different word related to the topic. If students repeat a word, or don't have one, then they must sit down and the game continues with the remaining players. The game finishes when there is one person standing.

Procedure:

1. Have students stand in a circle and assign a topic.

2. Clap your hands in a 1-2-3 beat and say the first word related to the topic.

3. Continue the rhythm and have the next student say a different word related to the topic. If students repeat a word or don't have one, they must sit down.

5. The game continues until there is one person left standing.

Make a Sentence

Skill: Writing

Time: 5 minutes

Age: 8+

Materials: Nothing, or worksheet/whiteboard/PowerPoint

To practice current or review vocabulary, have students make 1-5 sentences.

No Materials Version:

Have students use their books and choose a given number of words to make sentences.

Whiteboard/PowerPoint Version:

Give students a list of words to use all or some of.

Worksheet/PowerPoint Version:

Fill-in-the-blank or multiple choice with a word bank.

Procedure:

Begin with a brief oral review of the vocabulary words you want them to work with and elicit from the students what the words mean.

No Prep Version:

Have students take out their books and notebooks and tell them a number of sentences to make using those words. For example, "Turn to page 53 and choose three vocabulary words. In your notebook, write a new sentence using each word."

Whiteboard/PowerPoint Version:

Either give students a word list to choose from or, for lower-level classes, give them several sentences with a word bank. Have the students write the complete sentences in their notebooks.

Memory Circle Game

Skills: Speaking/Listening

Time: 5-10 minutes

Age: 6+

Materials: Nothing

This is a game that I often use with smaller classes of less than ten students. To set it up, you need to make a rule about what kind of words or grammar the students can use. Base it on whatever you are studying that day in class. For example: animals or past tense are good topics. You'll need to adjust the rules and criteria according to the level and age of your students. You want to make it challenging but not impossible so that everyone can have a chance to play at least once in a round. I'll use past tense for my example.

Have everyone stand up in a circle and begin the game by saying, for example, "I ate pizza." The next student says, "She ate pizza, and I studied English." The next student says, "She ate pizza, he studied English, and I watched TV." And so on it goes around the circle. If someone forgets someone or gets the order incorrect, he/she has to sit down and is out of the game. I usually let it go until there are 2-3 people left and then I give them a prize of some sort and start over with a new set of criteria.

If you have low-level students, a single word works better. For example, they can say "Cat," "Cat and dog," or "Cat, dog, and fish."

Teaching Tips:

You should participate in the game as well to impress students with your memory skills. It's a good way to end the game if it's taking too long—you go and declare the game finished!

Procedure:

1. Assign a topic or grammar point.

2. All the students stand up in a circle.

3. The first student says a word related to the topic.

4. The next student repeats the first word and a new word.

5. The third student repeats the first two words and adds a new one.

6. If a student misses a word, he/she sits down and is out of the game.

Steal the Eraser

Skills: Listening/Speaking

Time: 10-15 minutes

Age: 7+

Materials: 2 chairs, a table or desk, eraser

This game is a fun way to review grammar and vocabulary and makes an excellent activity for the class before a test. Divide the students into two teams. Have two desks at the front of the class facing each other with an eraser in the middle of the two desks. One student from each team comes and sits in the hot seat. Rotate through the class so that all the students get a chance to play at least once. You then ask a question of some sort, which you should prepare beforehand (one round = one question/2 students. Two rounds = one question/student. Include a few extras for a "bonus" round). The first person who grabs the eraser can try to answer the question. A helpful rule is that a student can take the eraser at any time, but you should stop talking as soon as someone touches the eraser. The student then has ten seconds to answer as you count down on your fingers. If the student is correct, he/she gets one point. If the student is incorrect, the other player gets a chance to answer the question after you repeat the full question one more time.

To make it even more exciting (or if one team is behind by a lot of points), you can have a "Bonus Round" where the teams pick their best three players and each question is worth three points.

Teaching Tips:

Emphasize that the first student to touch the eraser must take it in order to prevent any chaos. I also require students to keep their fingers on the edge of their desks when I begin the question. It's really important to stop talking the instant one student touches the eraser. If not, students will just grab the eraser and wait for you to finish the question, which is really unfair. It's best to use questions that have very well-defined answers so you don't have to make any judgment calls because half the class will be unhappy with you no matter what decision you make.

Procedure:

1. Prepare two desks facing each other at the front of the class, with an eraser in the middle.

2. Divide students into two teams.

3. Each team sends one person to the front to sit at the desks. I don't let students choose the person for each round but instead make them go in the order that they are sitting.

4. Begin asking a question (prepare the list beforehand), but stop speaking once the eraser is touched. Alternatively, you can have each team appoint a captain who takes turns reading the prepared list of questions in order to increase student talking time.

5. The first player to touch the eraser must answer the question within ten seconds. Count

down the time on your fingers.

6. If correct, he/she gets one point and the next two people come to the front for another question. If incorrect, read the question (in full) one more time and the opposing player gets a chance to answer the question within ten seconds.

7. If correct, he/she gets one point. If incorrect, both players sit down and the next pair comes up. You can share the correct answer with the class before saying a new question.

9. Continue until all students have had a chance to play at least once.

The Alphabet Game

Skills: Writing

Time: 5 minutes

Age: 7+

Materials: Nothing

This is a simple way to introduce a topic. Some examples include jobs, cities, animals, etc. Have pairs of students write down A~Z on one piece of paper. Give them 2-4 minutes to think of one word/letter that fits that certain category. I make a rule that they can't use proper nouns. If you want to increase the difficulty or if you have a small class, you can make a rule that if two teams have the same word it doesn't count. This forces students to think more creatively.

Example: Topic = animals

A. Alligator

B. Bat

C. Cat

Etc.

Procedure:

1. In pairs, students write down the alphabet on a piece of paper.

2. Give students a topic and a certain amount of time.

3. Students think of one word per letter about the topic.

4. Check who has the most words at the end of the allotted time. Option for small classes: don't count repeated words so students have to think more creatively.

Vocabulary Word Hunt

Skills: Reading/Writing

Time: 5-10 minutes

Age: 8+

Materials: Worksheet

Make a 3 x 3 grid with clues about nine vocabulary words and include a word bank. Have students use their dictionaries or glossaries to race to get 1/2/3 Bingos or complete the grid.

Here's an example of vocabulary word hunt: www.eslspeaking.org/vocabulary-word-hunt.

Procedure:

1. In advance, prepare 3 x 3 grids filled with clues about nine vocabulary words and a word bank.

2. Have students use their dictionaries or glossaries to get 1/2/3 Bingos or complete the grid.

3. The first student to correctly match the words with the definitions wins.

Word-Definition Match

Skills: Reading

Time: 5-10 minutes

Age: 7+

Materials: Cards or worksheet/whiteboard/PowerPoint

Card Version: Print one word or definition per card. You will need one set per student, pair or group. This version is good for pair/small group work and adds a speaking component to the task.

Worksheet/Whiteboard/PowerPoint Version: Create a word bank of current or review vocabulary and a list of definitions for students to draw a line (worksheet) or matching letters and numbers for whiteboard or PowerPoint.

Procedure (Card Version):

1. In advance, prepare cards with one word or definition per card. Print and laminate enough for each student, pair or group to have a set.

2. If you're having students work in pairs or small groups, divide the class accordingly and distribute a full set of cards to each. If students will be working alone, give each student a set of cards.

3. Have students match the words to their definitions as quickly as possible.

Procedure (Worksheet/Whiteboard/PowerPoint Version):

1. Have students match the words and definitions by drawing a line (worksheet) or matching letters and numbers and writing their answers in their notebooks.

2. Have students trade papers to check.

Games and Activities for Higher-Level Students

Dictogloss

Skills: Speaking/Listening

Time: 10-15 minutes

Age: 10+

Materials: A short story

This is a simple activity for higher-level students that helps them practice their listening and memory skills as well as substituting vocabulary words if the original word is no longer accessible to them. You can find a short, interesting story of some kind or make one up yourself. I've used various things: from children's stories to a story about something I did on the weekend. Just about anything can work.

Tell the story 1-3 times, depending on the student level, and you can vary your speaking speed to make this activity easier or harder. Once you are done telling the story, students will have to go in groups of 2-3 to retell the story. Emphasize that they won't be able to recreate the exact story that you told but that they should try their best to keep the meaning the same. Each team can pair up with another team to compare. Then, tell the original story again so students can see how they did.

This activity works well as a writing activity too.

Teaching Tips:

It's very helpful for students to compare answers with partners before they have to say anything in front of the class, so be sure to put them in pairs or groups of three to work together on this activity. It's useful for the weaker students to have a stronger student getting them up to speed. It also gives students confidence that they're on the right track, and they'll be less nervous to share their answers with the class.

If you use something "scandalous," it will make the activity a lot more fun! Of course, it should still be appropriate so just picture your boss observing your class to decide if you should use it or not.

Procedure:

1. Prepare a short story using the key vocabulary words that you'll read to your students.

2. Put students in groups of two or three and read the story to them.

3. Students try to remember the details of the story and compare with their group. I usually only allow them to do this by speaking.

4. Read the story again and have students attempt to recreate the story more closely, again by speaking.

5. Read the story again (depending on level and difficulty of story) and have students again attempt to recreate it even more closely.

6. Elicit a couple teams to tell their story to the class (in a small class). Alternatively, put two teams together and have them tell their stories to each other (in a larger class).

7. Read the story one final time for students to compare to their own.

-er Dictionary Activity

Skill: Reading/Writing/Speaking

Time: 10+ minutes

Age: 10+

Materials: Worksheet

Students learn early on that –er refers to a person who does something. Examples include teacher, writer, baker, etc. However, nouns ending in –er can refer to people, animals, or objects or can have multiple meanings involving a combination of the above. The activity will reinforce the need to be cautious with general rules in English while also providing dictionary practice.

Begin by preparing a list of nouns ending with –er. If you would like this to be a brief activity, limit it to about five words. The more words you include, the longer the activity will be. Have three columns beside the list for students to tick if the word refers to a person, animal, and/or object. Students should use their dictionaries to determine which categories each word belongs to.

Here are enough –er words for an entire class period:

Blender, Bumper, Buyer

Cadaver, Canister, Cleaner, Coaster, Customer

Diver, Dozer, Driver

Fryer

Hipster

Oyster

Passenger, Pitcher, Planner, Player

Ringer, Roster

Scanner, Sticker, Stinger

Walker

To add a speaking element, have students work with partners after filling in their answers. Partners should take turns asking and answering questions about the words. For example, "A person who bakes is a baker. Is a person who cooks a cooker?"

Teaching Tips:

Depending on the level of the class, you can give credit students who defend answers they may come up with, such as, "A banner is a person who bans," or you can explain that it is a logical conclusion, but even if English is not always logical.

This may be a good time to review "a person who. . ." and "a thing that. . ."

Procedure:

1. In advance, prepare a worksheet with a list of nouns ending in –er with tickbox columns for person, animal and object. Also, at least one class beforehand, instruct students to bring their dictionaries on the appropriate date, if you do not have class sets.

2. Explain to students that although they know that nouns ending in –er are people, -er words can also refer to animals and objects.

3. Have students use their dictionaries to categorize each word on the list as person, animal, and/or object.

4. When students have looked up all the words, have them work with a partner asking and answering questions about the words. For example, "Is a walker a person who walks?" (Answer: "Yes, and also something that helps people walk.")

Is that Sentence Correct?

Skills: Listening/Speaking/Writing

Time: 10-20 minutes

Age: 10+

Materials: Blank paper, vocabulary words

This is a sneaky way to get your students to make grammatically correct sentences using the target vocabulary. Start off by giving each student a different vocabulary word. It should be something that the students are quite familiar with already. The challenge in this activity is not the actual word; it's using it in a sentence. Give the students 2-4 minutes to make one sentence using that word. Do not offer any assistance or correct any errors.

The first student reads his/her sentence out loud to the class. All the other students must then vote whether it's correct or incorrect. Students make their own decision and there doesn't need to be a consensus. You make the final judgment about whether or not the sentence is correct, and if a student guessed correctly, he/she gets one point. If the sentence is incorrect, you can elicit some reasons why from the students. The next students read their sentences and the game continues.

Procedure:

1.Give each student a different vocabulary word.

2.Each student writes one sentence using that word.

3.The first student reads his/her sentence out loud to the class.

4.All the other students vote on whether it is correct or incorrect (students vote independently).

5.If the sentence is incorrect and a student voted "incorrect" he/she gets one point and vice versa. Students keep track of their total points.

6.If the sentence is incorrect, you can elicit reason why from the students.

Speaking Bingo

Skills: Speaking/Listening/Writing

Time: 20-30 minutes

Age: 10+

Materials: Blank "Bingo" grids/blank paper

This is a fun activity that teenagers as well as university students seem to love. Make a list of about 30 vocabulary words that you've been teaching. If you use less, the game will be over very quickly. Give the students a pre-made Bingo Grid or have them draw a 5x5 grid. Then, have students fill in the grid randomly from the list of words on the board or PowerPoint. Choose someone to go first (rocks-scissors-paper, draw numbers out of a hat, according to the attendance sheet, etc.). The first student describes a word but doesn't actually say the word. The next person describes another word and on it goes, just like a regular Bingo game except that the students are speaking the whole time. You can do variations, such as "1 line," "2 lines," "X-Bingo" and "Blackout." This variation works best in smaller classes of ten or less.

In bigger classes, you can describe the words but it becomes solely a listening and writing exercise instead of a speaking one. Another way to do it would be to put students in small groups of 4-6 to play together. There are two benefits: there's more student talking time, and it becomes more of a strategic game because each student can keep an eye on the opponent's boards.

Teaching Tips:

One important strategy to increase fluency that our students need to practice is producing synonyms of a word they don't know, or can't remember the exact one that they want. This Bingo game is an excellent way to focus on this.

This game requires absolutely no preparation time if you are given a class at the last minute and need something to fill the time. Ask the students what they've been studying the past few days or weeks and if they say "animals," for example then ask them to tell you all the animals they know. Write them on the board and that will form the list they have to choose from as they prepare their boards.

Ask the students to use a highlighter or just an "x" over the words instead of scribbling it out entirely with their pens. This way, you are able to check their answers in case of a Bingo.

Procedure:

1. Prepare blank Bingo grid photocopies beforehand (or have students draw their own on paper), as well as a list of vocabulary words (PowerPoint works well).

2. Students fill in the Bingo grid with their chosen words.

3. The first student chooses a word and describes it, using hints but not the word itself. You can choose the order of who describes words any number of ways: drawing numbers, seating arrangement, alphabetical order, etc.

4. All students cross off that word if they have it on their Bingo grid. The next student describes a word and so on.

5. The first student to get one line is the winner. The next winner is two lines, then "X," and then "blackout." My rule is that you can't win more than one round.

Vocabulary Apples to Apples

Skills: Listening/Speaking

Time: 30+ minutes, including deck-building

Age: 10+

Materials: Paper, pen/pencils, textbooks, scissors

Apples to Apples is a game in which players defend their choice of card played. This version is somewhat different than the actual Apples to Apples game in order to increase speaking time. Before playing, students need to make two decks of cards using vocabulary words. This is best done at the end of a semester or book so that there are more words to play with. You may also want to encourage them to brainstorm words they've learned previously.

For deck-building, divide the students into at least two groups: nouns and adjectives. If you have a large class, you may want to further divide them, for example, into person, place and thing groups. The groups should compile as many nouns and adjectives as they can. To keep the two decks easily identifiable, you can use two colors of paper or blank and ruled paper that has been cut into 8-10 pieces.

Collect the cards once the groups have finished creating them and keep the nouns and adjectives separate. Divide the class into groups of 5-8 students and have each group pick a judge. This person will be in charge of the decks of cards and also will have to choose the winner of each round. Each judge should be given an equal share of the two decks.

Have one group help you play a demonstration round in which you are the judge. Deal each group member five noun cards. Turn over one adjective card and have each student choose the noun card in his/her hand that best matches the adjective and give it to you. Read each card and have the students explain why their word is the best match. When all students have spoken, announce which card is the winner and why.

Have the judge in each group deal five noun cards to their groups and turn over/display one adjective card per round. Players must choose the noun card in his/her hand that he/she feels best matches that adjective and give it to the judge. The judge takes all of the noun cards and shows each card one at a time. Players must defend their card when the judge shows it.

Example:

If the judge draws the word "*big*," the other students may submit nouns like "*watermelon*," "*elephant*," "*heart*," and "*day*." The students can then defend their choices with a single sentence:

A: A watermelon is a big fruit.

B: An elephant is a big animal.

C: A kind person has a big heart.

D: An important day is a big one.

Encourage students to keep talking in order to convince the judge that their answer is the best.

When all players have spoken, the judge will decide the winner of that round. Each player will be given one more noun card by the judge. The judge will then give both decks to the winner of the round and that person becomes the new judge. He/she turns over the next adjective card to start the next round. If there are not many cards (vocabulary words) to play with, you may want to mix the discards back in to the live decks.

Teaching Tips:

While you can save a fair bit of class time by preparing the decks yourself, you can sneak in a bit of parts of speech review for students if they have to make the cards themselves. Additionally, as they are compiling the decks, students are also likely to come across words they have forgotten. This gives them a chance to discuss vocabulary with their teammates before the game begins (at which point their teammates will have little incentive to help.)

Procedure:

1. Before class, prepare cards by cutting sheets of colored printer paper into 8-10 pieces. Use two different colors.

2. Divide students into groups to build two decks of cards: nouns and adjectives. Students should use their textbooks and also brainstorm as many words as they can and write one word per card.

3. When the decks are ready, divide the students into groups of 5-8.

4. Divide the two decks equally between the groups and keep the two separate.

5. Have one group come to the front of the class to demonstrate. You will be the judge.

6. Turn over one adjective card. Have your group look at their cards, choose the noun that best matches the adjective, and give it to you.

7. Read each noun card and have the student who gave it to you defend his/her choice (see example above). Choose the best answer and tell the class why.

8. Have groups play rock-scissors-paper to choose the first judge for their group and play one round.

9. After each round, each player is dealt a new noun card, and the winner becomes the new judge (or you can have them rotate in a circle).

10.Used cards can be mixed back into the decks if there aren't many cards.

The Case for an Integrated Vocabulary Program

Vocabulary in ESL can be a strange animal, partly because some students really love to study it in isolation. This is particularly true when they are only studying English to get an all-important high test score. Other reasons why vocabulary is easy is because it is straight memorization, it can be studied alone and assessment couldn't be easier: you either know a word or you don't. Given that an individual's language fluency is often fraught with inconsistencies, knowing exactly where he or she stands can be quite reassuring.

However, no matter how fervently your students lobby for more vocabulary or, worse, ask about studying lists of words, there are pretty compelling reasons for integrating your vocabulary study as much as possible into your broader lessons. First, reading comprehension and vocabulary size have been connected in studies for decades. To state the obvious: you can't understand the content of a text if you don't know the words being used.

Reading comprehension relies on recognition of words, but even so, various studies have shown that between ten and forty exposures to a word are necessary for learning. The more your students read, the more words they will be see and the more quickly those words can become part of their working vocabulary.

Unfortunately, your students are pretty much guaranteed to feel sure they know a word (and will be sick of studying it) well before it has worked its way from short-term memory to working vocabulary. That's where this book comes in: using games and activities can disguise the same old thing as something, if not new and exciting, then something that is at least passably engaging.

A good vocabulary program will create an awareness of words as a single aspect of fluency. When planning a lesson, you should take into account using the terms in context, creating opportunities for multiple exposures to new terms using a mix of the four skills: speaking, reading, listening, and writing. Don't forget to activate prior knowledge to integrate new terms into their existing vocabulary, all while making it fun!

Don't get overwhelmed. Take a two-pronged approach: choose vocabulary based on usefulness to your students using the texts you have available and combine with the activities in this book to bring the fun. As always, recycle, recycle, recycle because learning a language is all about repetition.

Before You Go

If you found this book useful, please head on over to Amazon and leave a review. It will help other teachers like you find the book. Also be sure to check out my other books on Amazon at www.amazon.com/author/jackiebolen. There are plenty more ESL activities and games for children as well as adults.

CPSIA information can be obtained
at www.ICGtesting.com
Printed in the USA
LVOW04s0401090616

491768LV00028B/842/P